For:

_____

From:

_____

Date:

_____

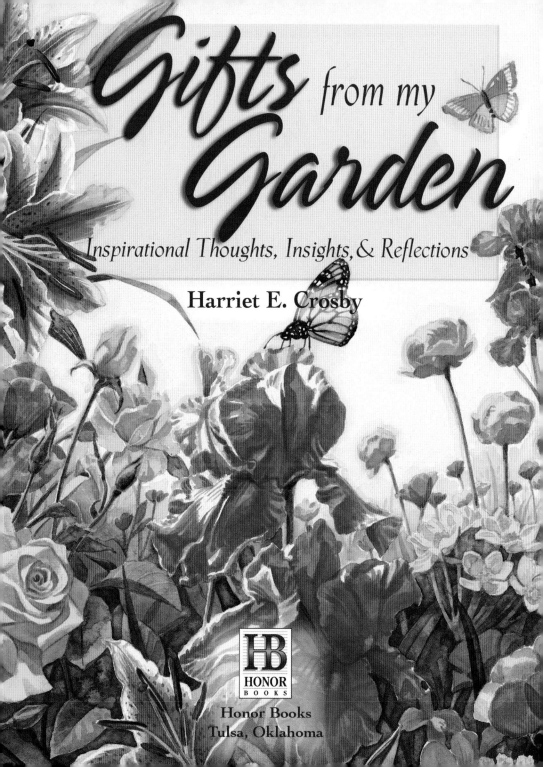

Gifts from my Garden

Inspirational Thoughts, Insights, & Reflections

Harriet E. Crosby

HB
HONOR
B O O K S

Honor Books
Tulsa, Oklahoma

Gifts from My Garden
ISBN 1-56292-853-8

Copyright © 2000 by GRQ Ink, Inc.
1948 Green Hills Boulevard
Franklin, Tennessee 37067

Published by Honor Books
P.O. Box 55388
Tulsa, Oklahoma 74155

Developed by GRQ Ink, Inc.
Cover design, interior design, and composition by Whisner Design Group, Tulsa, Oklahoma

Contributing illustrators: Taylor Bruce, Geyersville, California; Kelley Vandiver, Tulsa, Oklahoma

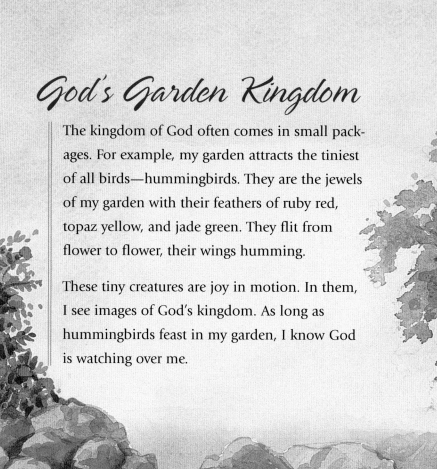

God's Garden Kingdom

The kingdom of God often comes in small packages. For example, my garden attracts the tiniest of all birds—hummingbirds. They are the jewels of my garden with their feathers of ruby red, topaz yellow, and jade green. They flit from flower to flower, their wings humming.

These tiny creatures are joy in motion. In them, I see images of God's kingdom. As long as hummingbirds feast in my garden, I know God is watching over me.

He was saying, "What is the
kingdom of God like, and to what
shall I compare it? It
is like a mustard
seed, which a man
took and threw into
his own garden; and
it grew and became a
tree, and THE BIRDS OF THE
AIR NESTED IN ITS BRANCHES."

LUKE 13:18-19 NAS

I rejoice, O God, to find Your kingdom in the
smallest of Your creation. And I rest in the
power of Your presence.

Amen.

God Gives Growth

I work hard in my garden. Planting, mulching, fertilizing, watering, pruning, weeding—it's a lot of work, but each activity is an act of love. And so my garden grows.

God works on me with even more care and diligence. He tends my soul, encourages my heart, heals my body, and feeds my mind—all because He loves me. And my spirit grows with gratitude.

I planted, Apollos watered,
but God gave the growth.

1 CORINTHIANS 3:6 NRSV

O God, to You alone, my Creator,
who gives growth to my
whole being, I offer up my thanks
and praise.

Amen.

A Gardener's Treasure

I know that each spring my garden will once again yield its hidden treasure. The bulbs I planted last fall poke their heads through the winter earth and bloom in glorious colors. Those spring flowers delight my winter-weary eyes.

Each of us is a hidden treasure in God's garden. He plants His Spirit within us, and it grows and prospers until our lives blossom and bloom in brilliant color. As He looks around at the work of His hands, I know He is delighted by what He sees.

The kingdom of heaven is like treasure hidden in a field, which a man found and hid; and for joy over it he goes and sells all that he has and buys that field.

MATTHEW 13:44 NKJV

O God, let me know Your touch
and feel the warmth of Your love
and approval.
Amen.

The Eternal Garden

When my mother died, it seemed as if someone flipped a switch, and my world was plunged into darkness. In spite of my grief, I kept up with my work in the garden because it was high summer and my flowers and plants needed water and care.

Slowly but surely, the beauty of my perishable garden began to reveal to me a wonderful truth. At the end of our lives, there is with God an imperishable world. And in that world, there is a garden—more beautiful than anything I could imagine. In it, I will once again meet my mother and all those who have gone on in faith before me. What joy and delight will be ours when we meet again.

So it is with the resurrection of the dead.
What is sown is perishable,
what is raised is imperishable.

1 CORINTHIANS 15:42 NRSV

In You, O God, is life without end.
Hallelujah!
Amen.

Joy in the Garden

Sometimes I come home at the end of a hard day with my shoulders and neck tied in knots. Stress is plentiful in our world. But then, I peek out at my garden and see a riot of roses—deep red, bright yellow, flaming orange, hot pink, even pale lilac. My burdens instantly begin to fall away.

My roses in full bloom provide a little taste of the wild joy of Heaven, where mountains sing and the trees clap their hands. Life's earthly rubble quietly slips away when exposed to the fierce beauty of these divine treasures.

You will go out in joy and be led forth in peace; the mountains and hills will burst into song before you, and all the trees of the field will clap their hands.

ISAIAH 55:12 NIV

O God, thank You for joy in my garden, this little taste of the wild joy that is to come.

Amen.

The Great Gardener

Sometimes in order to maintain the health and beauty of my garden, a diseased plant or a flower that no longer blooms must be uprooted and put into the compost pile. Death happens in my garden so that life will thrive more abundantly.

God, the Great Gardener, works life and death in me as well. He uproots weeds such as envy and anger so that flowers such as love and honesty can be sown in my heart. The uprooting is painful, but the result is more abundant life.

As for what you sow, you do not sow the body that is to be, but a bare seed, perhaps of wheat or of some other grain.

1 CORINTHIANS 15:37 NRSV

God, You are the Great Gardener. Uproot the dead and dying, that truth and beauty may abound in my life.

Amen.

Springtime of the Spirit

Spring has sprung! The air smells of freesia and hyacinth and mock orange blossoms. My garden is aflame with daffodils, tulips, and ornamental poppies. The soft fragrances and brilliant colors have given me spring fever. In fact, my spirit feels as if it could burst from my body and float on gentle breezes.

The time of singing has come—the time for life to be renewed in the earth. It is the time for bursting forth in joy and gladness. All praise be to God, the giver of Spring.

Flowers appear on the earth; the season of singing has come, the cooing of doves is heard in our land.

SONG OF SONGS 2:12 NIV

My heart sings Your praises, O God.
My spirit soars on Your wings.
Amen.

A New Garden

Winter is hard on me—especially February. The days are short, and it's too cold and wet to work in the garden. I sit in front of the fire and dream of spring. As the fire crackles and pops, I imagine lavender and cottage roses and columbine. I see visions of fat, red tomatoes ripening in my kitchen garden. I comfort myself that one day, perhaps by early April, my garden will sprout and grow, preparing to reward me with a magnificent harvest.

One day, under God's springtime, peace and joy and love will spring up before all of us. The long-awaited harvest will be more wonderful than anything we could have imagined. And I will leap for joy under an eternal, spring sun.

As the earth bringeth forth her bud, and as the garden causeth the things that are sown in it to spring forth; so the Lord GOD will cause righteousness and praise to spring forth before all the nations.

ISAIAH 61:11 KJV

O God, winter is here. But I know Your springtime is coming. May it come soon.

Amen.

Eden Revisited

Adam was a gardener—God made him so. And God has placed the same gift in me. I am most myself when I'm working in my garden paradise or sitting on my garden bench.

When I want to visit Eden, all I have to do is step out my back door. When I want to walk with God in the cool of the day, I follow my own garden path. What a glorious gift I have been given!

The LORD God took the
man and put him into the
garden of Eden to cultivate
it and keep it.

GENESIS 2:15 NAS

God, let me walk with
You in Eden today,
and let me know
the wonder of
Your love.
Amen.

The Sensual Garden

My garden is a sensual place. Its colors and shapes delight my eyes, and the birds that fly overhead are music to my ears. The luxuriant brush of rose petals against my skin takes my breath away—and oh, the fragrances my garden sends forth! Even my kitchen garden explodes with tastes and smells, colors and textures.

God gave me five senses with which to enjoy my life and the world around me. No wonder I sense His presence most intensely as I linger in my garden, gathering lilies.

My beloved is gone down into
his garden, to the beds of spices,
to feed in the gardens, and to
gather lilies.

SONG OF SOLOMON 6:2 KJV

Open my senses to You, O God.
Let me enjoy You in the beauty
of my garden.
Amen.

A Well-Watered Garden

During a particularly dark and frightening time in my life, a friend reminded me of God's promise to make me like a well-watered garden. What comfort is mine when I imagine my heart with an unfailing fountain bubbling and burbling in its midst, a symbol of God's unending joy.

But God's promise was not for me alone. All who wish to may partake of the powerful, life-giving waters that flow from God's throne. His comfort and joy are available to all who will open their hearts to receive.

The LORD will guide you always; he will satisfy your needs in a sun-scorched land and will strengthen your frame. You will be like a well-watered garden, like a spring whose waters never fail.

ISAIAH 58:11 NIV

O God, thank You that You make me like a well-watered garden, filled with Your unending joy.

Amen.

Weeding

There's a downside to spring in the garden—
weeds—and with weeds, timing is everything. I
like to pull them when they have grown big
enough for me to get a good grip but before
they fully mature and spread.

Weeds get into God's garden, too, and they grow
freely in the midst of the good crops God has
planted in me. He allows those weeds to grow
undisturbed until just the right moment. Then,
with my help, God the Good Gardener pulls
them one by one, leaving the garden of my heart
thriving and prosperous.

The owner's servants came to him and said,
"Sir, didn't you sow good seed in your field?
Where then did the weeds come from?"

MATTHEW 13:27 NIV

O God, help me not to worry over
the weeds I see in my life but to trust
in Your goodness and perfect timing.

Amen.

A Garden Blessing

In early spring, as I clean up after winter and begin planting, I say a blessing over my garden:

Bless the Lord, O my soul, and all that is within me, bless His holy name.

Bless this garden, O my Lord, so that all who come will know Your peace.

Bless the Lord, O my soul, and all that is within me, bless His holy name.

In peace and abundance, my garden will grow and prosper under God's hand of blessing. The garden of my heart will grow and prosper as well, for I have welcomed God's love into my heart to warm the soil and give life to the flowers He has planted.

Bless the LORD, O my soul,
and all that is within me,
bless his holy name.

PSALM 103:1 NRSV

Bless the Lord, O my soul.

Amen.

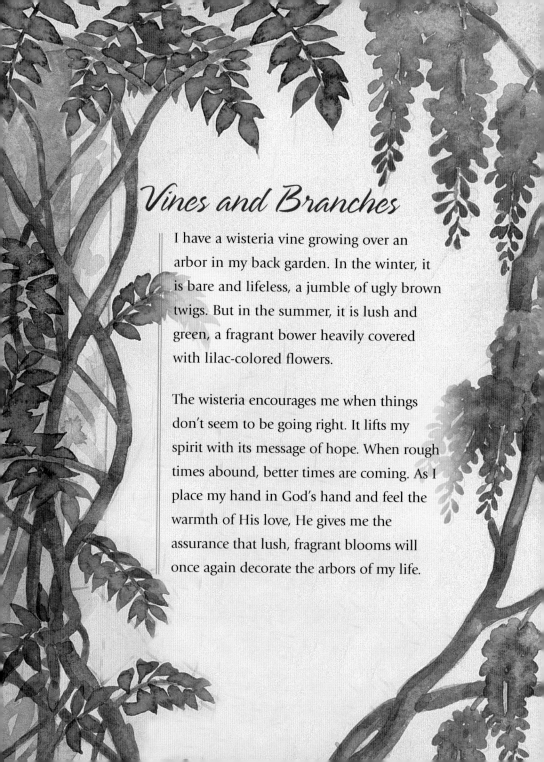

Vines and Branches

I have a wisteria vine growing over an arbor in my back garden. In the winter, it is bare and lifeless, a jumble of ugly brown twigs. But in the summer, it is lush and green, a fragrant bower heavily covered with lilac-colored flowers.

The wisteria encourages me when things don't seem to be going right. It lifts my spirit with its message of hope. When rough times abound, better times are coming. As I place my hand in God's hand and feel the warmth of His love, He gives me the assurance that lush, fragrant blooms will once again decorate the arbors of my life.

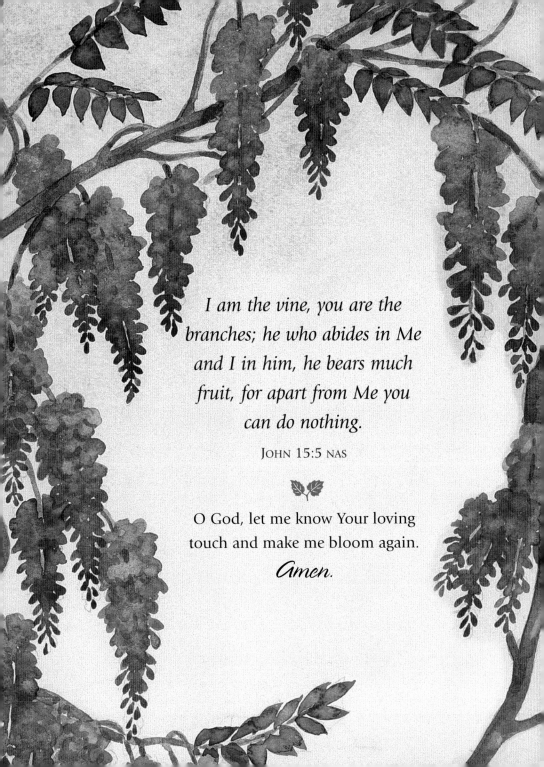

I am the vine, you are the branches; he who abides in Me and I in him, he bears much fruit, for apart from Me you can do nothing.

John 15:5 NAS

O God, let me know Your loving touch and make me bloom again.

Amen.

The Master Gardener

I spend too much time wanting—nicer clothes, a bigger house, a new car, a better job, more money, and on and on. What a waste of valuable time and energy!

My garden, my own little Eden, shows me that I already have enough and more than I need to live and enjoy life. The Master Gardener provides for me and gives me every good thing. I can stop my useless wanting—I have only to rest in the palm of God's hand.

The LORD God made all kinds of
trees grow out of the ground—trees
that were pleasing to the eye and good for
food. In the middle of the garden were the
tree of life and the tree of the knowledge
of good and evil.

GENESIS 2:9 NIV

O God, You give enough and more than
enough to enjoy this life. All praise to You.

Amen.

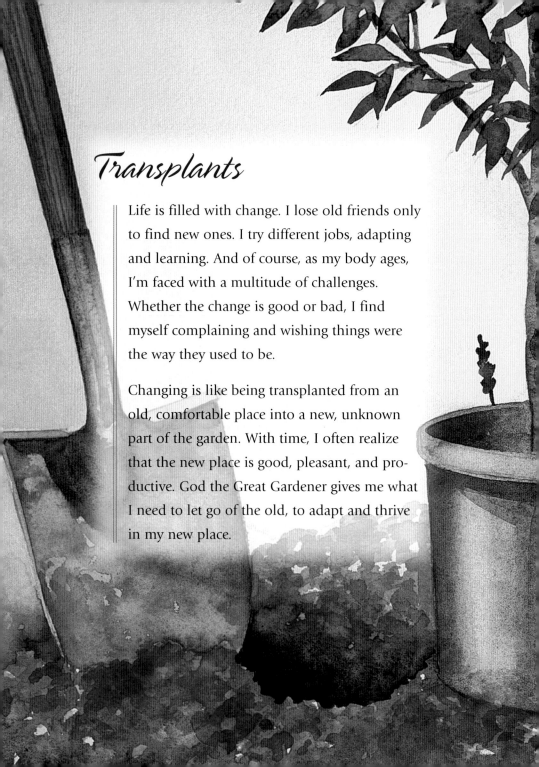

Transplants

Life is filled with change. I lose old friends only to find new ones. I try different jobs, adapting and learning. And of course, as my body ages, I'm faced with a multitude of challenges. Whether the change is good or bad, I find myself complaining and wishing things were the way they used to be.

Changing is like being transplanted from an old, comfortable place into a new, unknown part of the garden. With time, I often realize that the new place is good, pleasant, and productive. God the Great Gardener gives me what I need to let go of the old, to adapt and thrive in my new place.

*It was transplanted to good soil by
abundant waters, so that it might produce
branches and bear fruit and become a noble vine.*

EZEKIEL 17:8 NRSV

I'm in a new place in my life, O God. Help me
to let go of the old and adapt to this new
place that I may thrive and please You.

Amen.

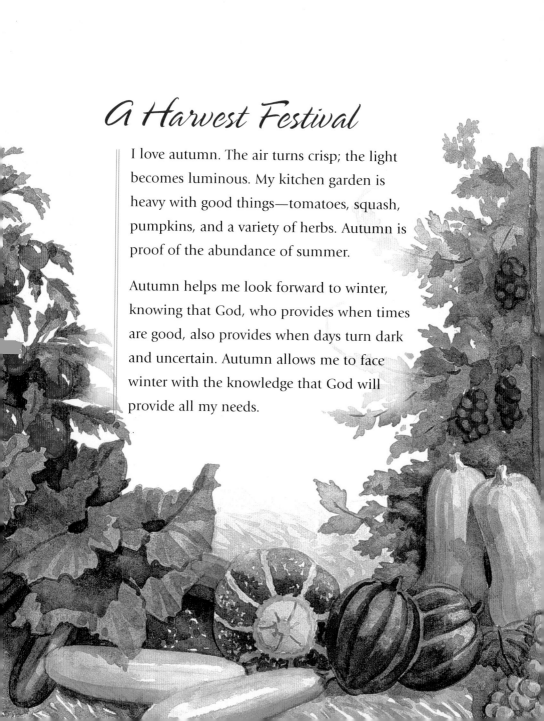

A Harvest Festival

I love autumn. The air turns crisp; the light becomes luminous. My kitchen garden is heavy with good things—tomatoes, squash, pumpkins, and a variety of herbs. Autumn is proof of the abundance of summer.

Autumn helps me look forward to winter, knowing that God, who provides when times are good, also provides when days turn dark and uncertain. Autumn allows me to face winter with the knowledge that God will provide all my needs.

*He who supplies seed to the sower
and bread for food will supply
and multiply your seed
for sowing and increase the harvest
of your righteousness.*

2 CORINTHIANS 9:10 NRSV

O God, as I harvest my garden,
continue to give me
whatever I need to see me through
the coming winter.

Amen.

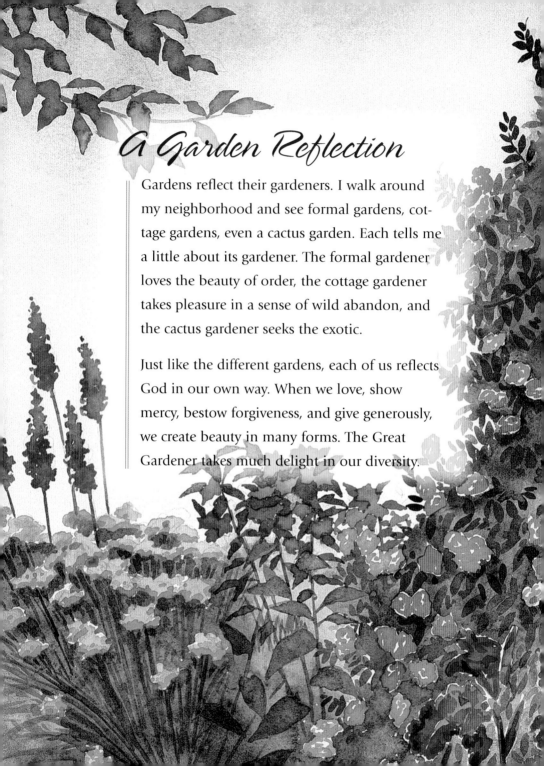

A Garden Reflection

Gardens reflect their gardeners. I walk around my neighborhood and see formal gardens, cottage gardens, even a cactus garden. Each tells me a little about its gardener. The formal gardener loves the beauty of order, the cottage gardener takes pleasure in a sense of wild abandon, and the cactus gardener seeks the exotic.

Just like the different gardens, each of us reflects God in our own way. When we love, show mercy, bestow forgiveness, and give generously, we create beauty in many forms. The Great Gardener takes much delight in our diversity.

*This is to my Father's glory, that
you bear much fruit, showing yourselves
to be my disciples.*

JOHN 15:8 NIV

O God, let me bear much fruit for You today,
that others might see You at work in my life.

Amen.

The Work of Faith

Hard work pays—especially in my kitchen garden. The herbs and vegetables I plant and labor over all spring and summer provide fresh, healthy, flavorful meals long into autumn. When October comes around, all the effort I've invested in my kitchen garden pays off.

The hard work of faith pays, too. Following after God, listening for His voice, and sensing His presence in my heart provide a rich harvest of assurance and courage when dark, uncertain times come.

He that tilleth his land shall be
satisfied with bread.

PROVERBS 12:11 KJV

Help me today to follow hard after You,
O God, so that my faith may grow.

Amen.

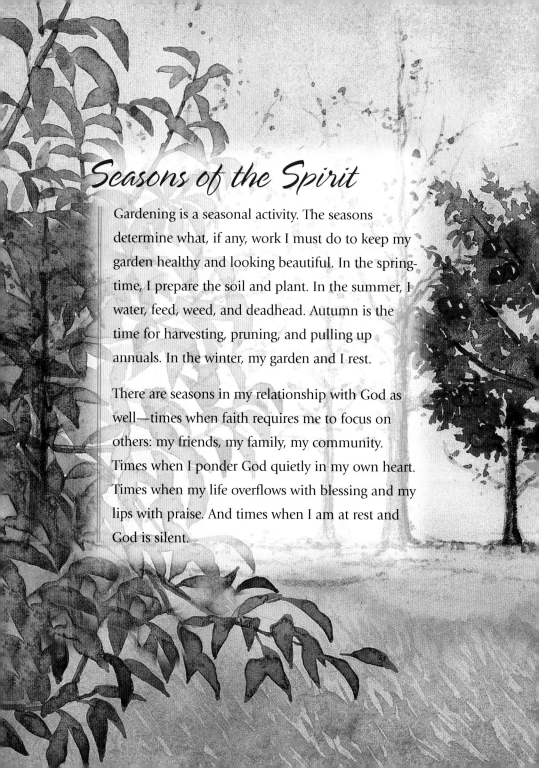

Seasons of the Spirit

Gardening is a seasonal activity. The seasons determine what, if any, work I must do to keep my garden healthy and looking beautiful. In the spring-time, I prepare the soil and plant. In the summer, I water, feed, weed, and deadhead. Autumn is the time for harvesting, pruning, and pulling up annuals. In the winter, my garden and I rest.

There are seasons in my relationship with God as well—times when faith requires me to focus on others: my friends, my family, my community. Times when I ponder God quietly in my own heart. Times when my life overflows with blessing and my lips with praise. And times when I am at rest and God is silent.

For everything there is a season, and a time for every matter under heaven: a time to be born, and a time to die; a time to plant, and a time to pluck up what is planted.

ECCLESIASTES 3:1-2 NRSV

O God, help me to faithfully honor the seasons
You have placed in my life.

Amen.

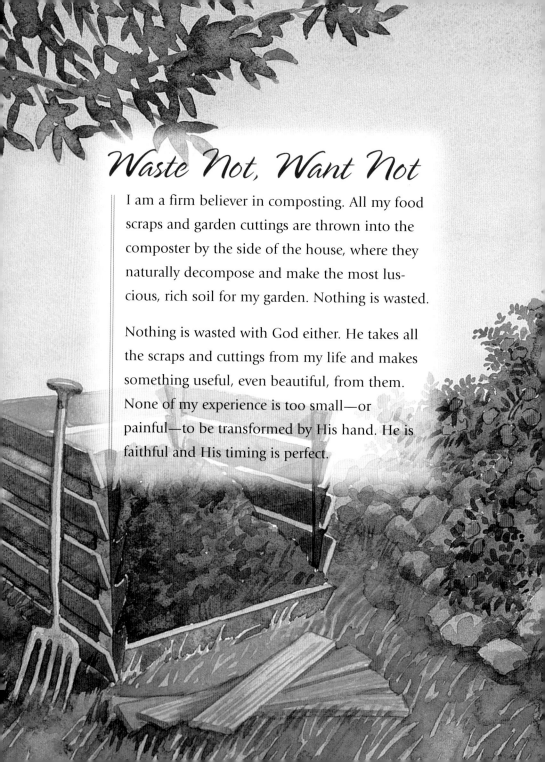

Waste Not, Want Not

I am a firm believer in composting. All my food scraps and garden cuttings are thrown into the composter by the side of the house, where they naturally decompose and make the most luscious, rich soil for my garden. Nothing is wasted.

Nothing is wasted with God either. He takes all the scraps and cuttings from my life and makes something useful, even beautiful, from them. None of my experience is too small—or painful—to be transformed by His hand. He is faithful and His timing is perfect.

When you reap the harvest of your land,
moreover, you shall not reap to the very
corners of your field nor gather the gleaning of
your harvest; you are to leave them for the
needy and the alien. I am the
LORD your God.

LEVITICUS 23:22 NAS

Let me see today that none of my
experience is a waste, O God, but is
transformed into something
beautiful by faith.

Amen.

Gently in the Garden

I worked hard today in my garden—a lot of digging and planting and heavy lifting. Just as the sun began to set, I took my cup of tea and went out to look over my work. The air was soft and cool, and the setting sun made my garden glow. It was a gentle, quiet time that warmed and uplifted my soul.

My heart is filled with thankfulness today as I am reminded of a great truth. One day, God, my shepherd, will lead me to a gentle and lovely garden place, which He has prepared especially for me.

Shepherd your people with your staff, the
flock of your inheritance, which lives by
itself in a forest, in fertile pasturelands.
Let them feed in Bashan and Gilead
as in days long ago.

MICAH 7:14 NIV

Lead me gently, O God, to Your eternal garden,
and let me bask in the glow of Your love.

Amen.

A Different Orchard

I have a friend who has a small orchard behind his home. Strolling through it one summer day, I was amazed by its bounty—pears, apples, plums, citrus trees, even avocados. I remember thinking, *He'll never go hungry with an orchard like this—and neither will the neighborhood!*

I want my life to bear its own kind of fruit. As I follow God, I pray that my heart will become a kind of spiritual orchard, providing a harvest of love, forgiveness, and generosity. I pray, too, that my family, my friends, and all those I encounter each day will be blessed by the treasure they find there.

*Bear fruit in keeping
with repentance.*

MATTHEW 3:8 NAS

O God, make my heart
a place rich with the
fruit of Your presence
in my life.

Amen.

A Garden Oasis

Gardens are often sanctuaries. When I'm in a world of hurt and pain, I head instinctively for my garden. It is an oasis, a balm for the ache in my soul. Give me a trowel or a pair of hand pruners, and let me get to work. After a while, I can feel myself relax as I am strengthened and encouraged.

Jesus Christ, our Lord, headed instinctively to a garden shortly before His suffering began. The Garden of Gethsemene must have felt like an oasis in the midst of a world of trouble as He knelt to pray. We are told that He left the Garden strengthened and ready to do all His Father had called Him to do.

*When Jesus had spoken these words, he went
forth with his disciples over the brook Cedron,
where was a garden, into the which he
entered, and his disciples.*

JOHN 18:1 KJV

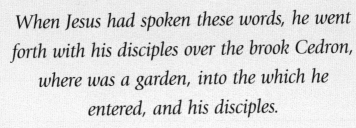

O God, make my garden an oasis
where You heal my soul.

Amen.

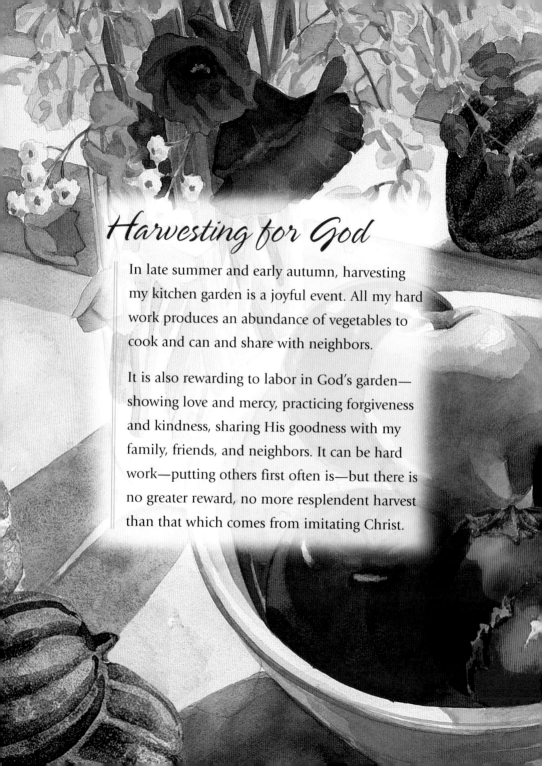

Harvesting for God

In late summer and early autumn, harvesting my kitchen garden is a joyful event. All my hard work produces an abundance of vegetables to cook and can and share with neighbors.

It is also rewarding to labor in God's garden—showing love and mercy, practicing forgiveness and kindness, sharing His goodness with my family, friends, and neighbors. It can be hard work—putting others first often is—but there is no greater reward, no more resplendent harvest than that which comes from imitating Christ.

He said to them, "The harvest is plentiful, but the laborers are few; therefore ask the Lord of the harvest to send out laborers into his harvest."

LUKE 10:2 NRSV

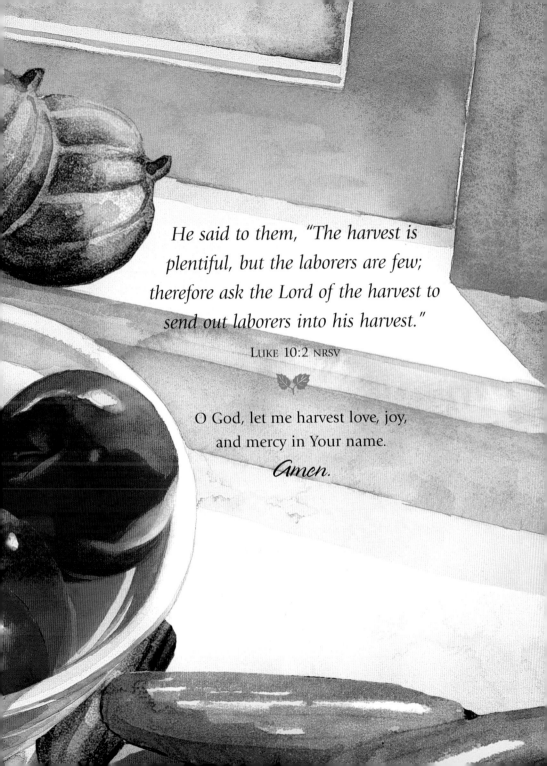

O God, let me harvest love, joy, and mercy in Your name.

Amen.

Garden Solitude

Sometimes I need to be alone—away from friends and family and the demands of my life. I crave the stillness necessary to hear God's voice.

When solitude is what I need, I pick up my pruning shears and head to my garden to pray and listen. In the garden, I'm alone, but never lonely. For God watches over me, and we talk quietly until my heart is content.

After he had dismissed them, he
went up on a mountainside by
himself to pray. When evening
came, he was there alone.

MATTHEW 14:23 NIV

Thank You, Lord, for the solitude that
allows me to hear Your precious voice.
Amen.

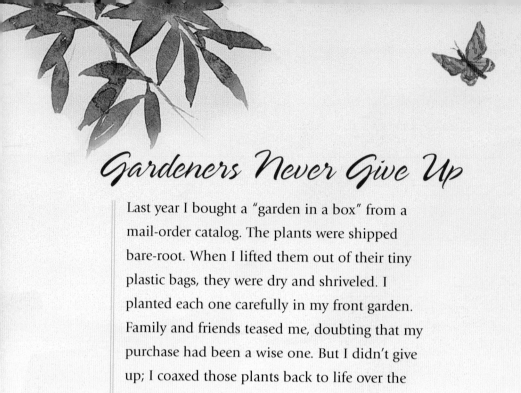

Gardeners Never Give Up

Last year I bought a "garden in a box" from a mail-order catalog. The plants were shipped bare-root. When I lifted them out of their tiny plastic bags, they were dry and shriveled. I planted each one carefully in my front garden. Family and friends teased me, doubting that my purchase had been a wise one. But I didn't give up; I coaxed those plants back to life over the next several weeks. And to my great delight, they are now thriving.

When I'm tempted to give up, I am reminded that God wants me to persevere. Sometimes it's the only way to bring my dreams back to life and cause them to thrive again.

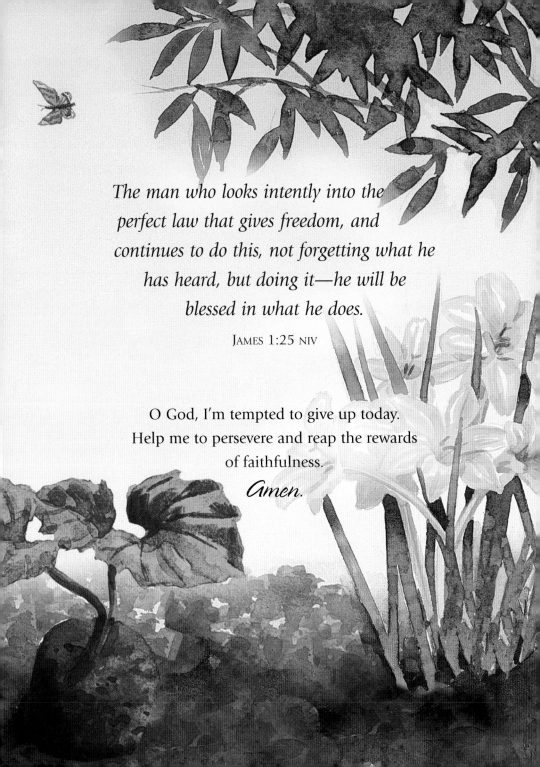

*The man who looks intently into the
perfect law that gives freedom, and
continues to do this, not forgetting what he
has heard, but doing it—he will be
blessed in what he does.*

JAMES 1:25 NIV

O God, I'm tempted to give up today.
Help me to persevere and reap the rewards
of faithfulness.
Amen.

Dirty Hands, Clean Heart

When there's dirt under my fingernails and my hands are plunged into the soil, planting or weeding or harvesting, my heart is singing to God.

Perhaps it is reaching down into the matter of God's awesome creation that makes me consider His goodness and my place in the scheme of things. I feel humbled and privileged to be part of His great plan. And I can't help but cry out to Him, asking for a clean heart that I might better sing His praises.

Create in me a clean heart, O God, and
put a new and right spirit within me.

PSALM 51:10 NRSV

Create in me a clean heart,
O God, for I rejoice in Your creation.
Amen.

Garden Animals

The birdbath in my garden attracts juncos, finches, robins, jays, California towhees, cedar waxwings—even an occasional deer. These creatures are a constant reminder that God is a faithful provider.

I see how simply their needs are met, and I am encouraged that He will also meet my needs. I see how carefree and happy they are, and I am inspired to throw aside my worries and rejoice in the hope of His provision. How could God forget me when He has not forgotten even one of these lovely creatures?

Are not five sparrows sold for two pennies?
Yet not one of them is forgotten by God.

LUKE 12:6 NIV

O God, in Your mercy, remember me
and hear my prayer.

Amen.

Listening in the Garden

I find I pay more attention to sounds when I'm at work in my garden—the sound of birds singing, my neighbor mowing his lawn, even the occasional jet flying high overhead.

I am also more attentive to the whisper of the great shepherd standing near me. And I hear love speaking softly. I hear mercy's gentle voice. I hear grace welcoming me into God's presence.

He is our God; and we are the
people of his pasture, and
the sheep of his hand.

PSALM 95:7 KJV

O God, let me listen
to Your voice as
I listen to birdsong.
Amen.

The Humble Garden

I have a T-shirt that says Every Garden Counts. The words are printed over a picture of a spade and pitchfork. A garden may be several acres large or as small as an African violet in its pot, but make no mistake, even the humblest garden is beautiful to God.

Faith is beautiful to God as well. No matter how great or small my faith may be, He is always pleased when I walk humbly beside Him, trusting in His love and mercy and finding rest for my soul. Every garden counts—including the garden God grows in my heart.

*Take my yoke upon you and
learn from me, for I am gentle
and humble in heart, and you
will find rest for your souls.*

MATTHEW 11:29 NIV

I come humbly, seeking rest for my soul,
O God. Let me rest in Your gentleness.

Amen.

Garden Optimists

A couple of weeks ago, I found a miniature rosebush trying to grow beneath an enormous lavender bush. It was tiny and scraggly and sort of ugly. It looked pretty sick, but I transplanted that rosebush to a better spot and continued to feed and water it. I trimmed off the ugly, dead leaves—eternally optimistic that when summer arrives, I'll be blessed with tiny, vibrant blooms.

God is eternally optimistic about me, too. He trims off the ugly, dead leaves in my soul. It doesn't feel good, but I know it's for my best. Then He feeds me with His goodness and gives me living water to drink, confident that I, too, will one day vibrantly bloom.

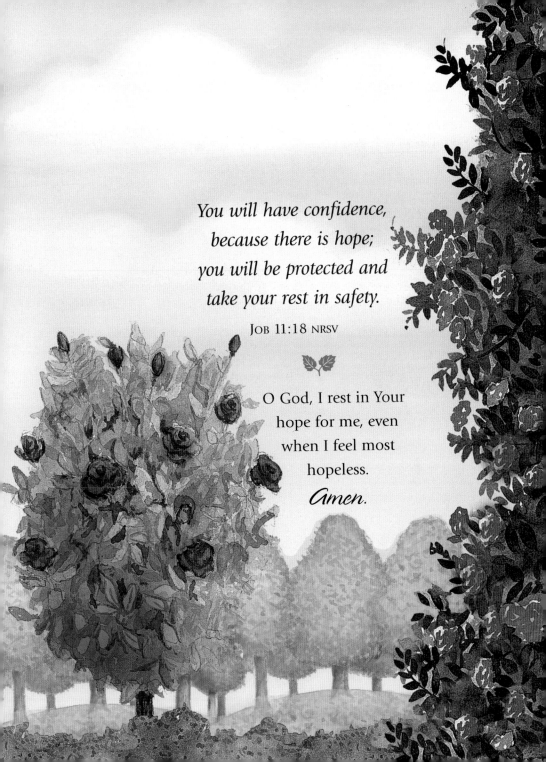

You will have confidence,
because there is hope;
you will be protected and
take your rest in safety.

JOB 11:18 NRSV

O God, I rest in Your
hope for me, even
when I feel most
hopeless.
Amen.

Breathing in the Garden

Sometimes I get so wound up and tied in knots that I find myself taking puny little breaths of air that only make me more tense. The shallower the breath, the more anxious I feel. Full, round breathing helps dispel stress and relax tense, worried muscles. Relief often comes as I work in my garden.

As soon as I begin to work, my breathing slows and becomes deeper. Slowly but surely, tense muscles relax as fresh oxygen reaches them. And I can feel the breath of God's Spirit upon me, whispering words of peace.

*The spirit of God hath made me, and the
breath of the Almighty hath given me life.*

JOB 33:4 KJV

Slow me down, Lord, and let me breathe
deeply of Your Spirit again.

Amen.

A Wintry Garden

One of my garden magazines has pictures of a garden covered with snow. It is beautiful. The graceful trees, bushes, and garden furniture are dusted in white, reminding me of fine lace.

The garden of my heart is sometimes covered with snow as well. Those are the seasons when God is silent. When I pray, there is no answer. But God's silence is beautiful in its own way. It is holy and majestic. In the winter seasons, I have learned to wait in holy silence as complex and, in its own way, as lovely as lace.

As the days of a tree, so will be the days of my people; my chosen ones will long enjoy the works of their hands.

ISAIAH 65:22 NIV

O God, we have come to a wintry place, You and I.
Help me to rest in the beauty of Your silence.

Amen.

The Indoor Garden

In the depths of winter, when nothing grows outside, I turn to my orchid garden, which grows inside. With proper care, I can coax these beauties to bloom two or three times a year. Even in winter, my house is filled with exotic blooms.

God cares for my inner garden, just as I care for my orchids. Even when my needs are not apparent on the outside, He is at work, nurturing and caring for me on the inside. When I pause to turn inward and reflect, I can see the lovely blooms my soul is producing.

*He carved the walls of the house
all around about with carved
engravings of cherubim, palm
trees, and open flowers, in
the inner and outer rooms.*

1 KINGS 6:29 NRSV

O God, though nothing grows
on the outside, I rejoice to see
You at work in my soul's garden.

Amen.

Garden Meditation

On cloudless summer mornings, I like to lie in bed, listening to birdsong. Often a breeze will touch my garden wind chimes and set them to singing. A whole new day, ripe with endless possibilities and adventures, beckons me.

On matchless mornings like these, I am certain that the breath of God still moves over this beautiful planet. I know, too, that the Spirit of God is lifting me up to meet each new challenge. I feel as if I am being borne aloft on the wings of angels.

I lay down and slept; I awoke,
for the LORD *sustains me.*

PSALM 3:5 NAS

O God, I lie down and sleep;
I wake again, for You sustain me.
Amen.

Gardens Cure Anxiety

When I'm worried and anxious, I watch the birds in my garden. They scratch the ground for seeds and insects and splash about in the birdbath. They haven't a care in the world because God provides all they need.

Worry changes nothing. It only spoils the precious moments I have been given in this life. Instead, I will go into my garden and watch the birds at play.

Look at the birds of the air; they do not sow or reap or store away in barns, and yet your heavenly Father feeds them. Are you not much more valuable than they?

MATTHEW 6:26 NIV

Take away my worries, O God,
and let me rest in
Your care for me.
Amen.

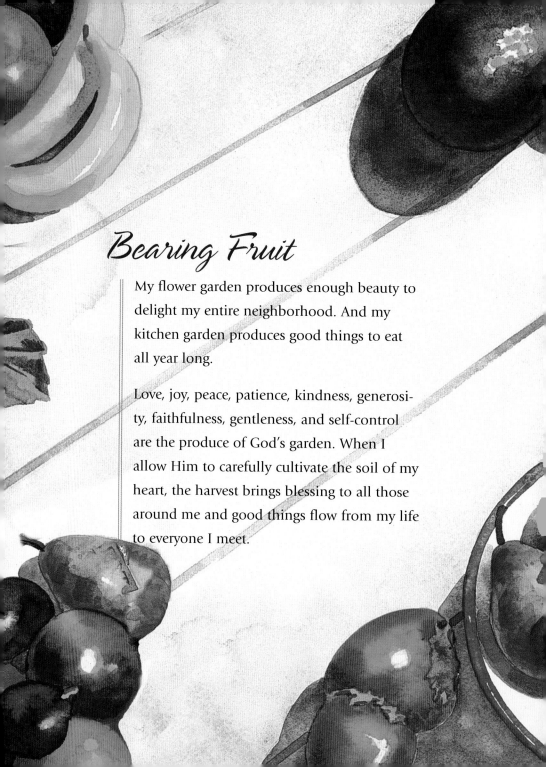

Bearing Fruit

My flower garden produces enough beauty to delight my entire neighborhood. And my kitchen garden produces good things to eat all year long.

Love, joy, peace, patience, kindness, generosity, faithfulness, gentleness, and self-control are the produce of God's garden. When I allow Him to carefully cultivate the soil of my heart, the harvest brings blessing to all those around me and good things flow from my life to everyone I meet.

O taste and see that the LORD is good.

PSALM 34:8 NRSV

May Your Spirit bear fruit in me today, O God.

Amen.

The Last Word

The world is filled with bad news. It would be easy to slip into despair as I hear of all the terrible things happening each day.

But I have only to look at my garden, and I am instantly reassured that God's creation is good. One day, the darkness will be banished once and for all. Beauty and virtue will abound. My garden tells me, again and again, that God has defeated every foe.

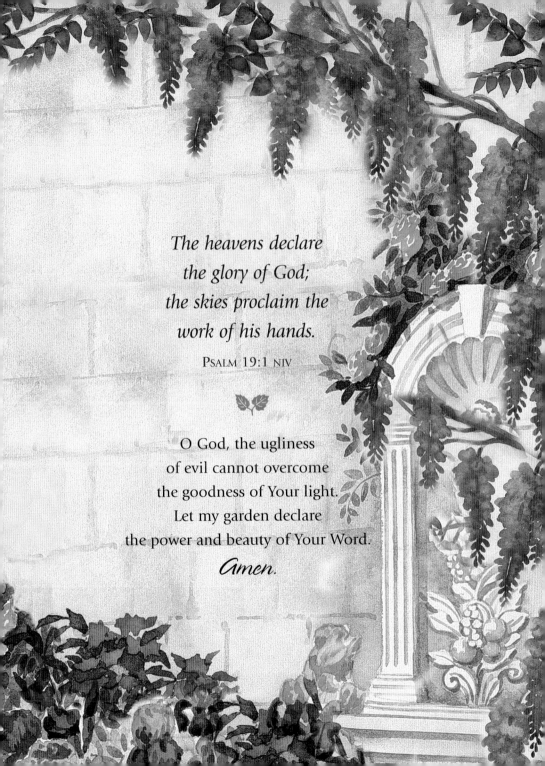

The heavens declare
the glory of God;
the skies proclaim the
work of his hands.

PSALM 19:1 NIV

O God, the ugliness
of evil cannot overcome
the goodness of Your light.
Let my garden declare
the power and beauty of Your Word.
Amen.

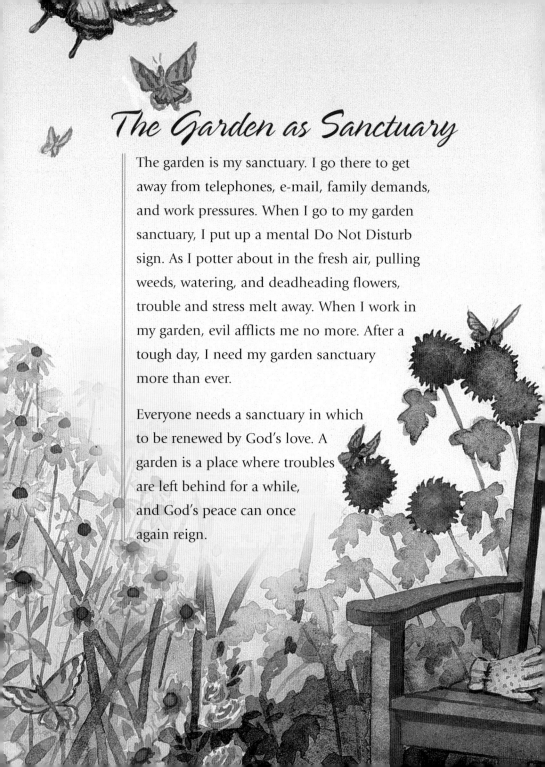

The Garden as Sanctuary

The garden is my sanctuary. I go there to get away from telephones, e-mail, family demands, and work pressures. When I go to my garden sanctuary, I put up a mental Do Not Disturb sign. As I potter about in the fresh air, pulling weeds, watering, and deadheading flowers, trouble and stress melt away. When I work in my garden, evil afflicts me no more. After a tough day, I need my garden sanctuary more than ever.

Everyone needs a sanctuary in which to be renewed by God's love. A garden is a place where troubles are left behind for a while, and God's peace can once again reign.

One thing I asked of the LORD, that will
I seek after: to live in the house of the LORD all the
days of my life, to behold the beauty of the LORD,
and to inquire in his temple.

Psalm 27:4 NRSV

God, You have given me my garden as a sanctuary.
Cover me with Your mercy as the shade of a tree
covers the ground underneath.

Amen.

Coping with Drought

Here, in California, the threat of drought is one that every gardener faces. Recently I replaced my water-hungry front lawn with a garden filled exclusively with drought-tolerant plants. Now, rain or shine, my garden will always bloom.

The garden of my heart is also subject to drought—those times when my passion for spiritual things fades. Prayer helps me stay drought tolerant. When I bow my heart in prayer, God is always faithful to pour out His living water on my parched soul. Slowly but surely, the act of prayer restores and nourishes me.

As a deer longs for flowing streams, so my
soul longs for you, O God.
My soul thirsts for God, for the living God.

PSALM 42:1-2 NRSV

God, my soul is dry. My spirit thirsts for You.
Help me in this time of drought. Help
my prayers to be like flowing streams
through this dry season.

Amen.

The First Gardener

At the end of the summer, I sit on my front porch and survey my garden. A year ago only dead grass and weeds existed in my front yard. Now my eyes behold a variety of colorful flowers blooming beside vibrant, healthy shrubs. Hummingbirds, butterflies, and bees dance about them. My garden now teems with beauty and life.

I know how Adam must have felt as he took care of Eden—proud of his hard work yet humbled by the beauty of God's creation.

The LORD God took the man
and put him in the garden of
Eden to till it and keep it.

GENESIS 2:15 NRSV

God, You have given me my own little
Eden to till and keep. Thank You for the
strength You give me to work my
garden and for the beauty that
delights all Your creatures.
Amen.

Growing Faith

Not long ago I sowed tiny catnip seeds in my garden. One small seed grew into an impossibly large three-and-a-half-foot bush, which was four feet in diameter. All the cats in the neighborhood came to nest in its branches.

Faith as small as a mustard seed, or a catnip seed, can do big and impossible things. When faced with problems that threaten to overwhelm me, I harvest a few catnip leaves to give to the cats and thank God. For I know that, with His help, I can move mountains.

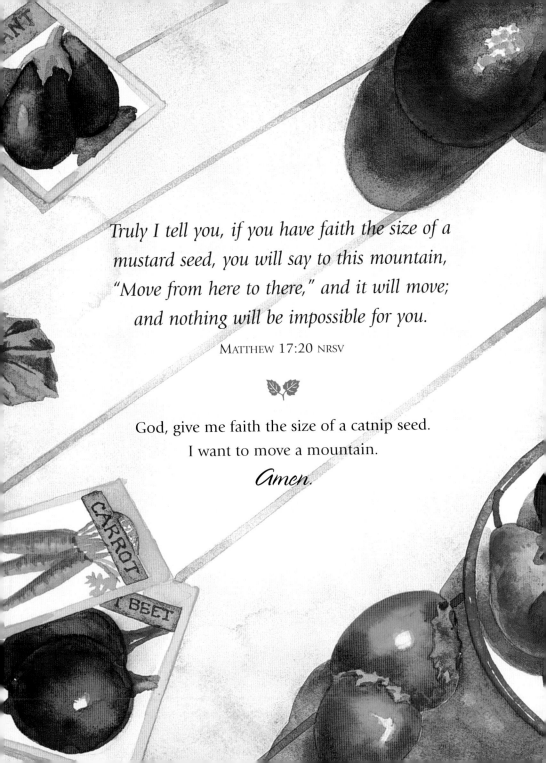

Truly I tell you, if you have faith the size of a mustard seed, you will say to this mountain, "Move from here to there," and it will move; and nothing will be impossible for you.

MATTHEW 17:20 NRSV

God, give me faith the size of a catnip seed.
I want to move a mountain.

Amen.

We Give Thanks

It is Thanksgiving. The sky is overcast
and a wind is blowing; more snow is
predicted by nightfall. Inside, all is cozy
and warm. A fire burns in the fireplace.
A fine Thanksgiving luncheon—complete
with the last vegetables from my kitchen
garden—graces the dining room table.

Any minute, family and friends will
gather around. I bow my head for just a
moment. "What more could I possibly
ask, O Lord. Thank You."

You shall eat in the presence of the LORD your God.

DEUTERONOMY 14:23 NAS

O God, for all of Your beauty,
and for all of Your love and
mercy, make me truly grateful.
Amen.

If you have enjoyed this book, you will also enjoy other gift books available from your local bookstore.

Gifts from My Front Porch
Letters from God
Letters from God for Teens
Daily Blessings for My Secret Pal
Daily Blessings for My Wife
Daily Blessings for My Husband
Lighthouse Psalms
Garden Psalms
Love Psalms
Psalms for Women

If this book has impacted your life,
we would like to hear from you.

Please contact us at:
Honor Books
Department E
P.O. Box 55388
Tulsa, Oklahoma 74155

Or by e-mail at:
info@honorbooks.com